The Instructors Guide To Playing Guitar !

Over the years many of my students would ask me if there were books available that I could recommend which would help them in their progress. So I have put a two book series together that will take the beginner right through to becoming a competent guitar player. Sure there are many books on the market that just cover chords, however what I wanted was a no-nonsense book that would take the absolute beginner right through to becoming a confident guitar player and to include all levels of players in between.

I have divided the course into two books, it is important not to move on to Book 2, until you are completely competent with Book 1. I want them to be easy to follow and get the student playing music as quickly as possible.

The books cater for all levels, from beginner right up to the accomplished guitar player and is a useful tool for those who feel qualified and confident enough to give guitar lessons, it also covers both left and right handed players. If you enjoy music then playing the guitar can be a very enjoyable activity at all levels.   **Good Luck!**

Cathal R. Gogan.

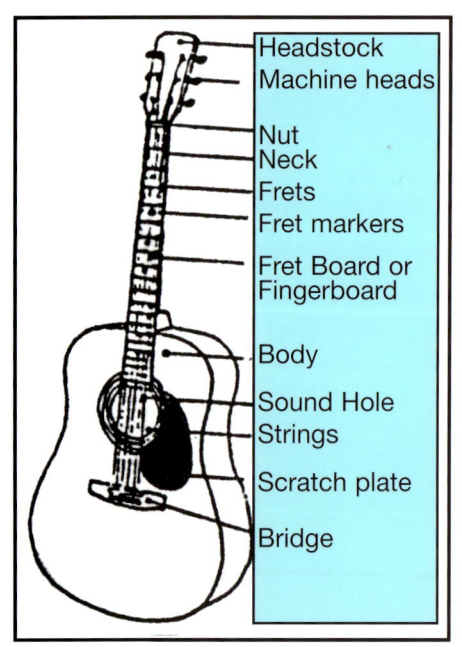 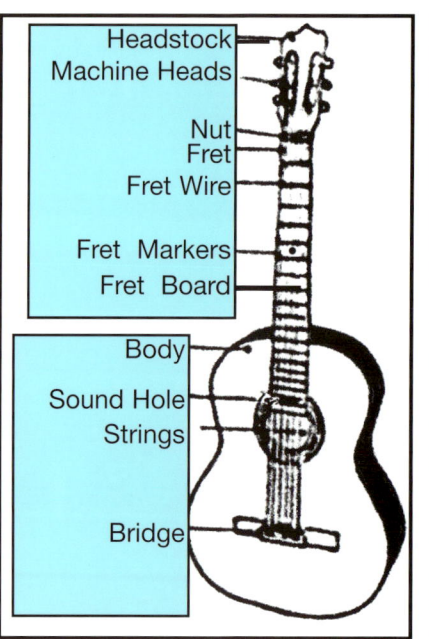 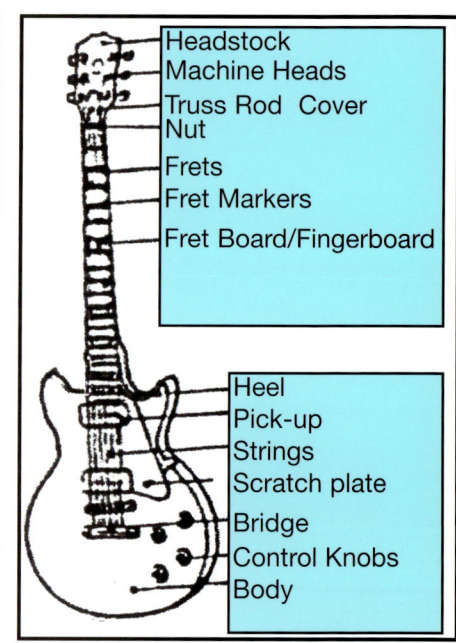

Acoustic Guitar **Classical Guitar** **Electric Guitar**

There are three main types of guitar each giving three very distinctive sounds, your choice of instrument will depend on the type of music you wish to play.
1   The **Acoustic Guitar** or sometimes called the Western Guitar for Modern, Folk, Ballad and Country music.
2   The **Classical Guitar** or sometimes called the Spanish Guitar for Classical, Flamenco and Latin types of music.
3   The **Electric Guitar** for Jazz, Country, Rock, Rhythm and Blues,

The **Acoustic Guitar** is the most common guitar that people will start on, it is very varied in the types of music that you can play on it.
It has steel strings which give a very sharp and distinctive sound and is a very versatile instrument. Learning to play it for the first few weeks will be hard on your fingers due to the steel strings but your finger tips will harden after a couple of weeks of practice and should not bother you after that.

The **Classical Guitar** gives a softer sound due to the nylon strings, it is best suited to Flamenco and Classical music.
The fret board is wider than the Acoustic and Electric Guitar so if you have been playing either for a while the Classical Guitar will take a while to get used to. You will notice that there is no scratch plate on the Classical Guitar, this is due to the style and method of playing music on it.

The **Electric Guitar** can only be played when connected to an amplifier, it has small microphones called pick-ups, which pick-up the sound from under the strings and sends it through to the amplifier, it is a very popular instrument and gives a wide and varied controlled sound. The chords are easier to hold down than the Classical and the Acoustic Guitar especially when playing bar chords.

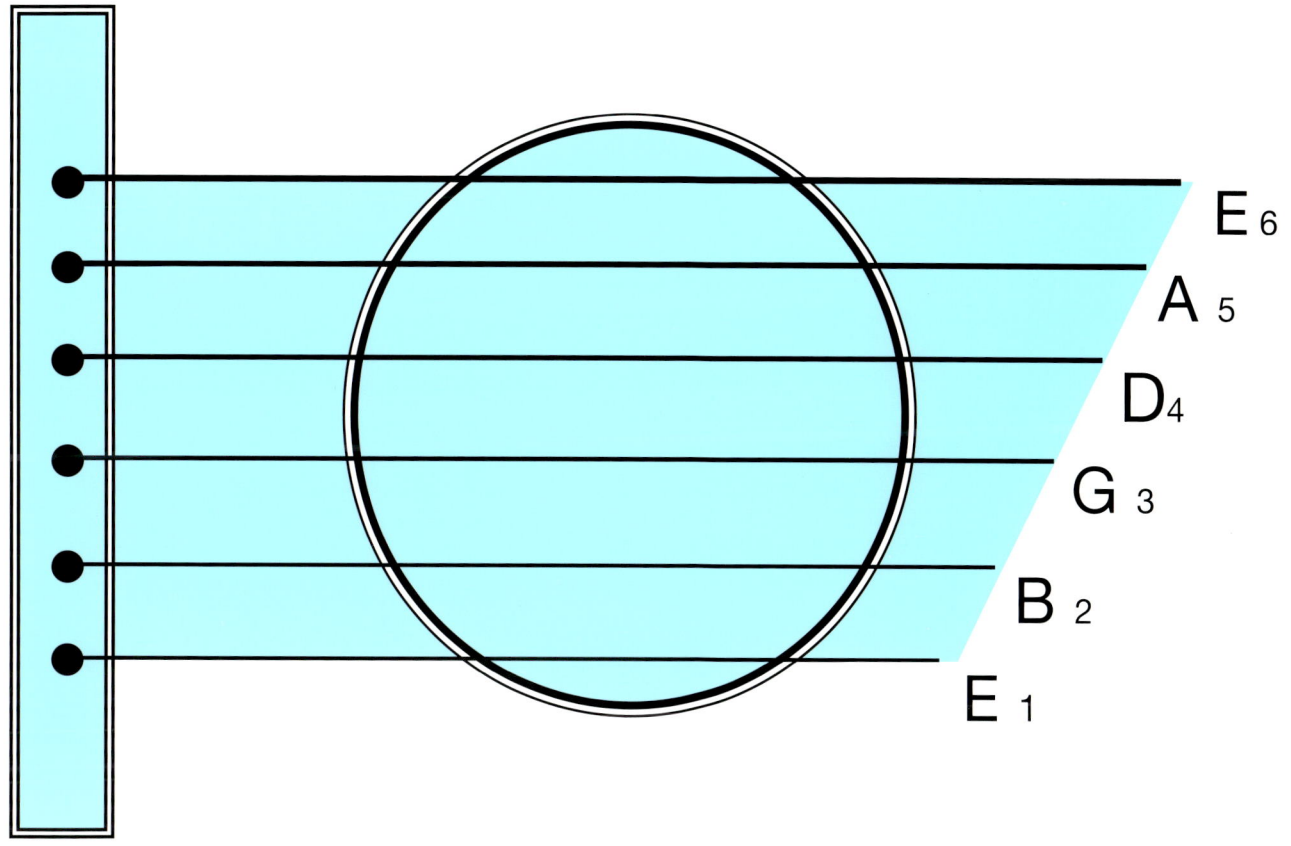

The Strings

On the standard guitar there are six strings:
The top string is an **E string** sometimes called the E 6, it's the 6th string from the bottom and the thickest and heaviest string on the guitar. It gives those lovely bass sounds that we get when we play our chords.

The **A string** the 5th. from the bottom also gives us our bass notes
The **D string** is next and the 4th. from the bottom, it's a middle string and gives us our middle sound between the bass and treble sounds
The **G string** is the 3rd. from the bottom and is also a middle sounding string.
The **B string** is 2nd. from the bottom and is a treble sounding string with its higher pitch notes.
The **E string** is the 1st. string and also gives us our higher pitch treble sounds. You will notice that there are two **E strings** the top and Bottom.
So we have

E.	6	Top	————————
A.	5		————————
D.	4		————————
G.	3		————————
B.	2		————————
E.	1	Bottom	————————

The bottom **E1 String** is the narrowest but you will notice after tuning it gives us the same E sound as the **top E6 String** which is the heaviest.

The strings can be purchased as Heavy Gauge, Medium Gauge, Light Gauge and Extra Light Gauge.
On the Acoustic guitar for beginners I would recommend the **Extra Light** or the **Light Gauge,** they will be easier to hold down chords and kinder to the tops of your fingers.
It is important to replace the strings on your Acoustic Guitar with similar Acoustic Guitar strings as the Electric Guitar and Classical Guitar strings will not be compatible with the Acoustic Guitar and vice versa.

Now for Tuning
All noise that hits our ears is made up of melodic sounds including our speech, its those high and low sounds that we refine and convert into music. The strings are tuned to sounds, the E sound, the A sound the D sound, the G sound, the B sound there are two E strings so the bottom is also an E sound.
We tune the Guitar by means of an Electronic Tuner. Tuners are very easy to use and relatively inexpensive, a very consistent and reliable way to tune your guitar, they are a must have for beginners. Most of them operate on a red and green light system or two red lights followed by a bleep when the sound hits the right pitch, ask the sales people for a quick run-down on the tuner at the point of purchase.

The old method of tuning was by means of a pitch pipes, you would blow the pipes similar to a miniature mouth-organ and tune each string to each of the six notes on the pipes, It was not always very accurate especially for the beginner.
As you become confident in your guitar playing you will get familiar with the sounds and rely less and less on your tuner.

I once heard a famous guitarist say that "**Tuning a guitar is always a compromise and getting it 100% correct was more luck than skill** " well that may have been true in the past, but with the modern tuners available on the market these days it cuts out the guesswork and you should certainly get it in tune as closely as possible to 100% percent.

Playing Notes and Chords

We play the guitar by means of notes and chords out of which our music is played. A chord is a collection of notes from which collective sounds are made, a single string played or plucked is called a note, where one finger is placed in any position on the fret board and played you will get a single note, the single note that you will get will be a note from A to G, if more than one finger is placed and all the strings are played together then it is called a chord. The chords will also be from the A chord to the G.chord.

The chords on the following pages are played by putting the appropriate finger on the string in the appropriate position. So fingers 1, 2, 3, 4, (shown beside) the thumb is not included as this is placed at the back of the fret board. It is important to use the right fingers in the right positions as this will make it easier to move to the next chord while being played in the course of a song or a piece of music.

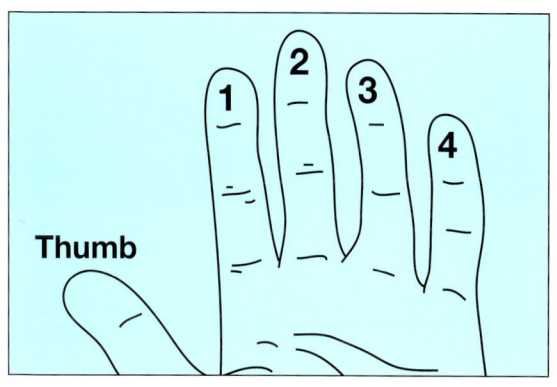

I have included a page listing all the *Major Chords A to G.*
All the *Minor Chords A to G.* And all the *7ths A to G. (Tick them off as you get familiar with them.)*
There are no H Chords or notes nothing comes after the Gs. So you see A - G is seven full notes and on the eight full note you are back to an A note this is called an **Octave** or **Eight Note** which will sound the same as the A note that you started with only it will be at a higher Pitch.
The same goes for the rest of the notes if you start at a **D note** as example below your eight note will bring you on to a **D note** only at a higher Pitch.

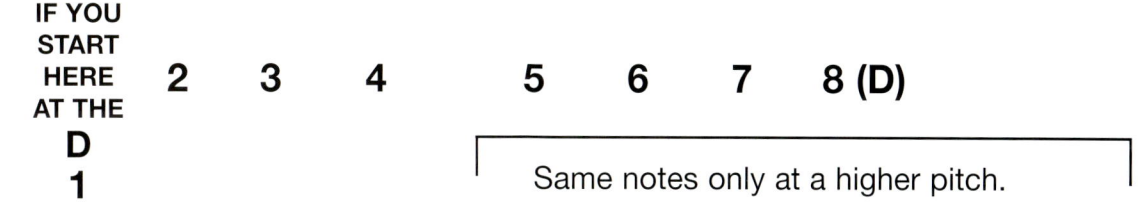

Normal Pitch notes from tuning

(See Pages 24 & 25) for further explanation

The notes in bold print above are the notes that six of our Guitar Strings are tuned to E. A. D. G. B. E.

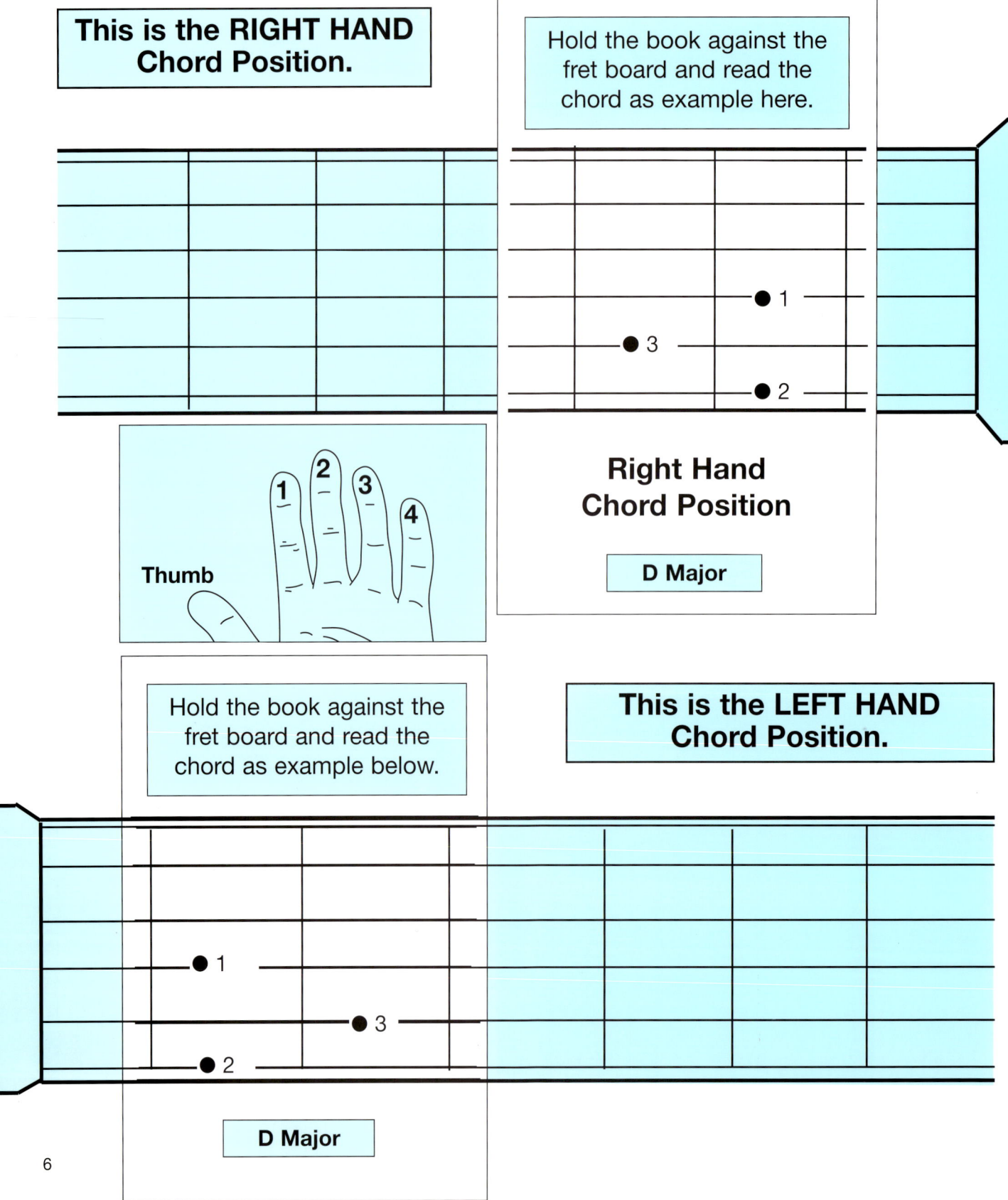

Major Chords
A B C D E F G

Minor Chords
Am Bm Cm Dm Em Fm Gm

Sevenths (7ths)
A7 B7 C7 D7 E7 F7 G7

'Don't try to learn all of these chords at once. Start with the **A,s** spend a week on them until you are getting a good clean sound, then move to the **D,s**. as the **Bs** and **C,s** contain Bar Chords.
After the **D,s** try the **E,s** followed by the **C,s** the **G,s**. and **B,s**. last of all the **F,s**.
Chords **B,s C,s F,s** and **G,s** all contain bar Chords.

A **Barre Chord** is where your first finger is used as a bar to cover all of the strings, considerable force is needed to hold down the chord and it takes a bit of practice before you will get a good clean sound. (**Don't worry you will get it with practice!**)

How to read the chords for LEFT HANDED Players Only

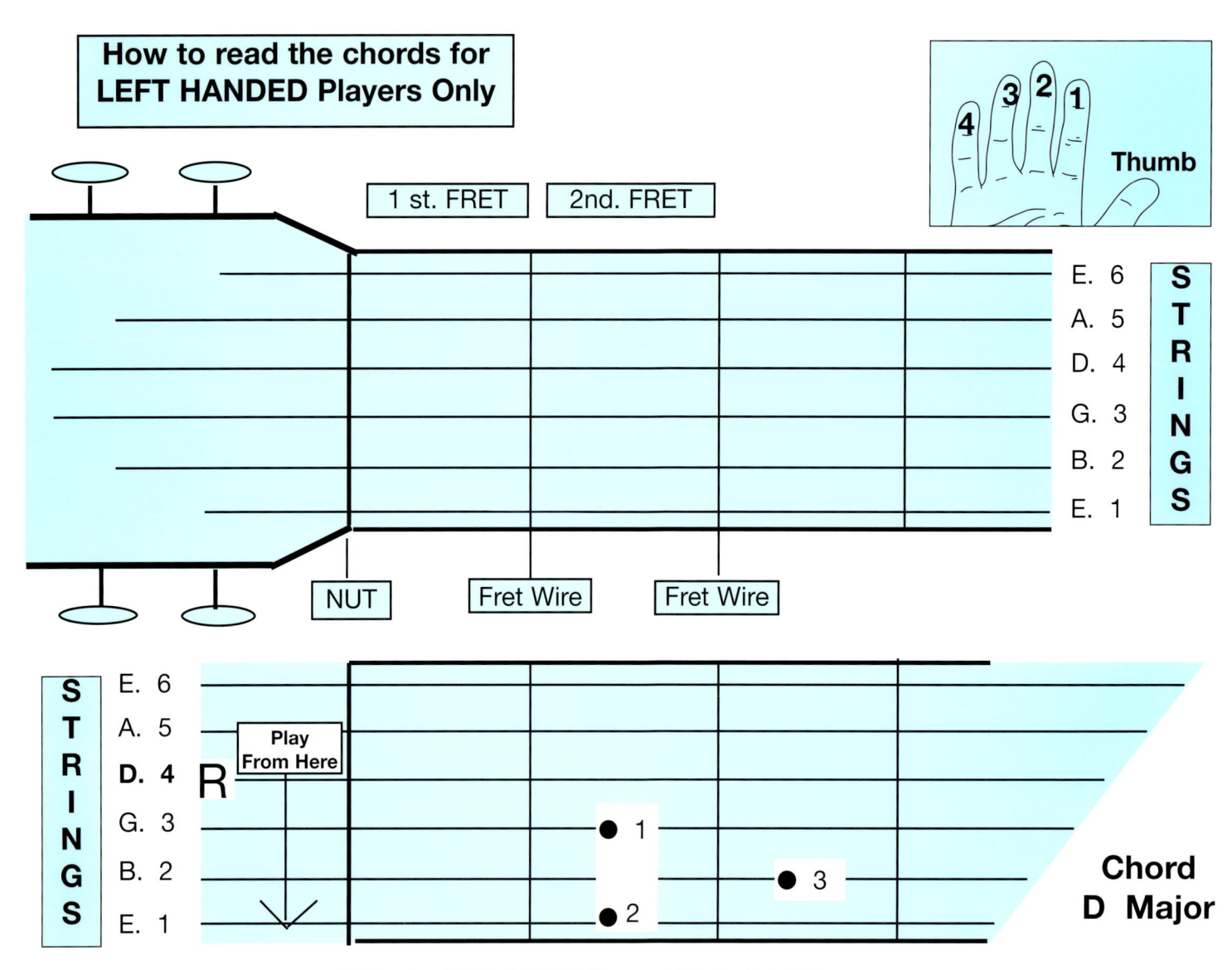

1st. FRET   **2nd. FRET**

E. 6
A. 5
D. 4
G. 3
B. 2
E. 1

STRINGS

Thumb

NUT   Fret Wire   Fret Wire

STRINGS

E. 6
A. 5
D. 4   R   Play From Here
G. 3
B. 2
E. 1

Chord D Major

Start playing from the string which contains the **R** and continue to the bottom string as in the D Major chord here.
The string with the **R** is called the **ROOT NOTE** of the chord it will be the same note (D) as the chord (D) you are playing and will vary from chord to chord. (Important) You cannot hit the strings above the **R** while playing a Chord.

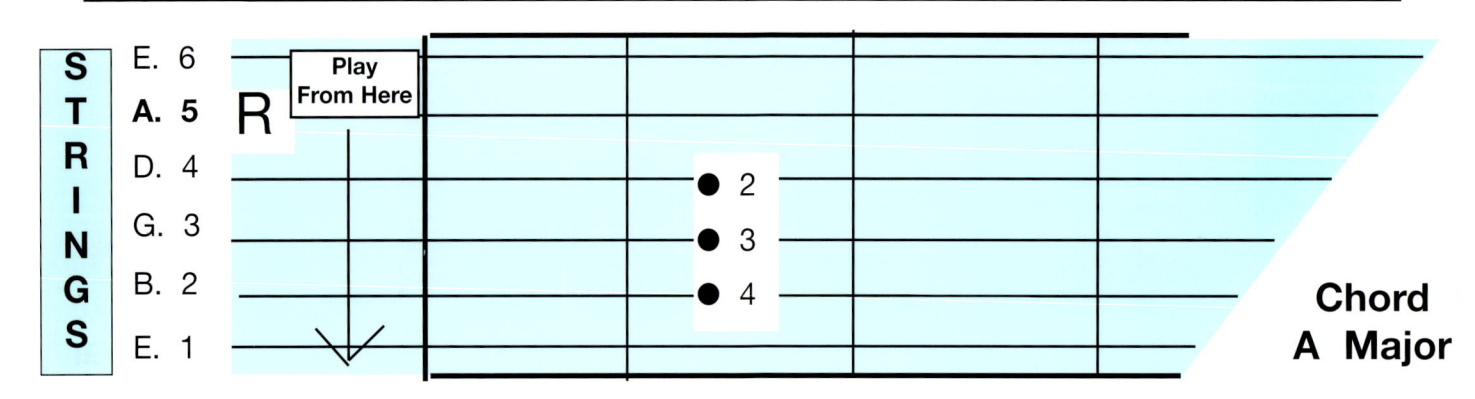

STRINGS

E. 6
A. 5   R   Play From Here
D. 4
G. 3
B. 2
E. 1

Chord A Major

See example here for the **A Major** playing from the **A String**

IMPORTANT
If you write and do most activities with your left hand, then you will play the guitar using left chord positions as above and on the following left hand page columns only.

8

How to read the chords for RIGHT HANDED Players only

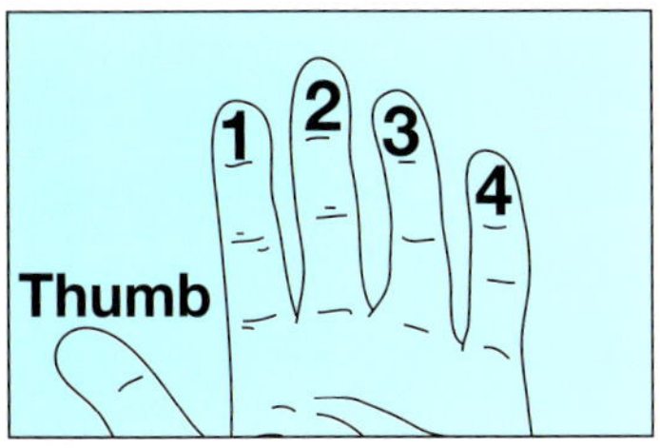

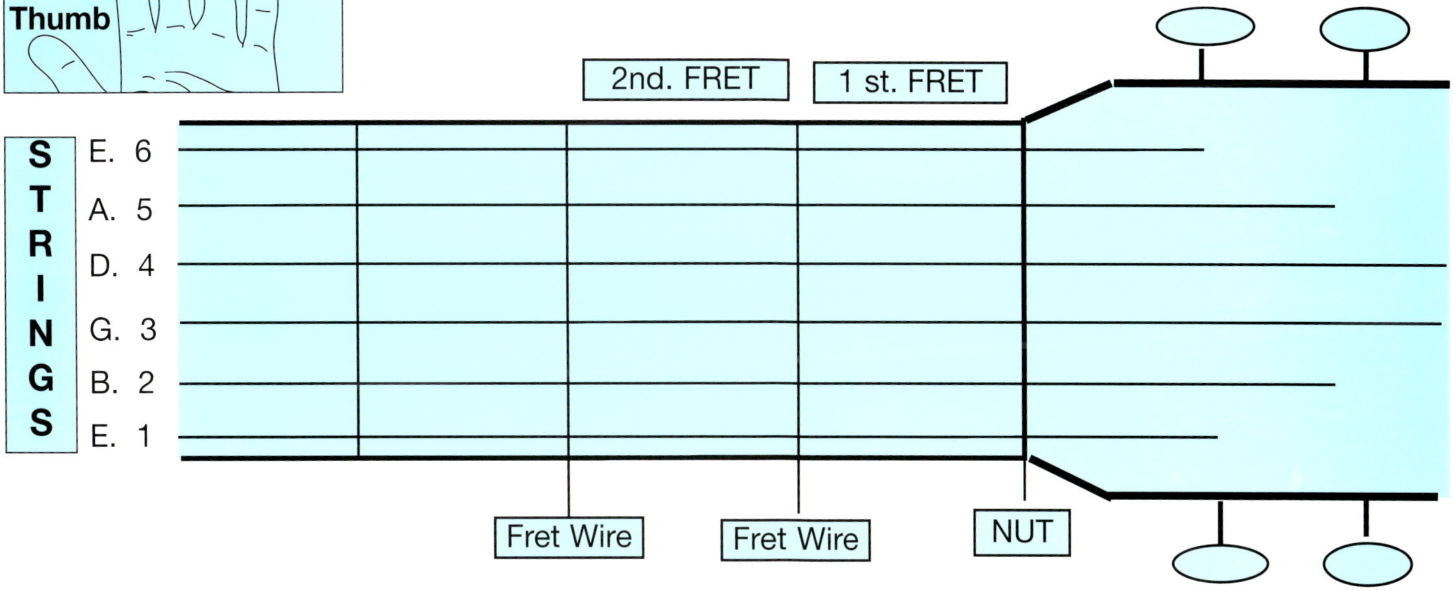

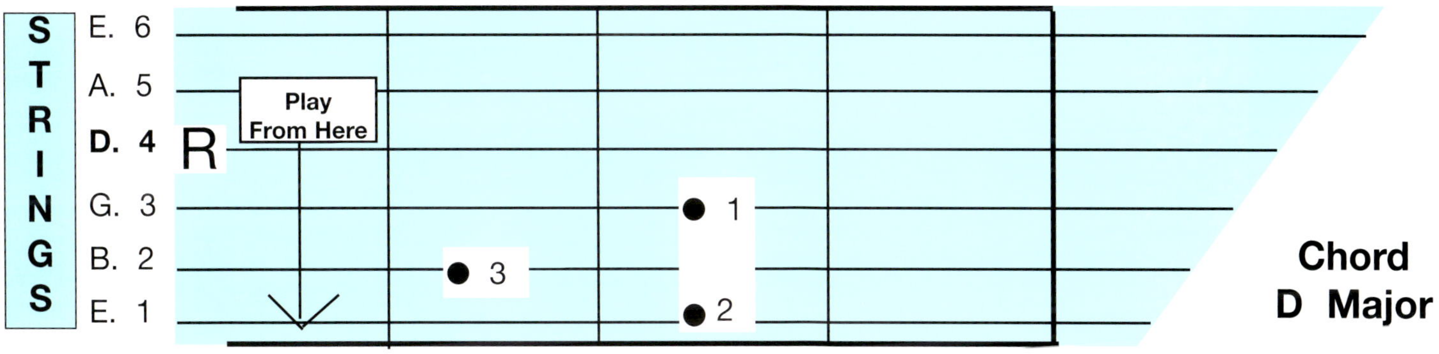

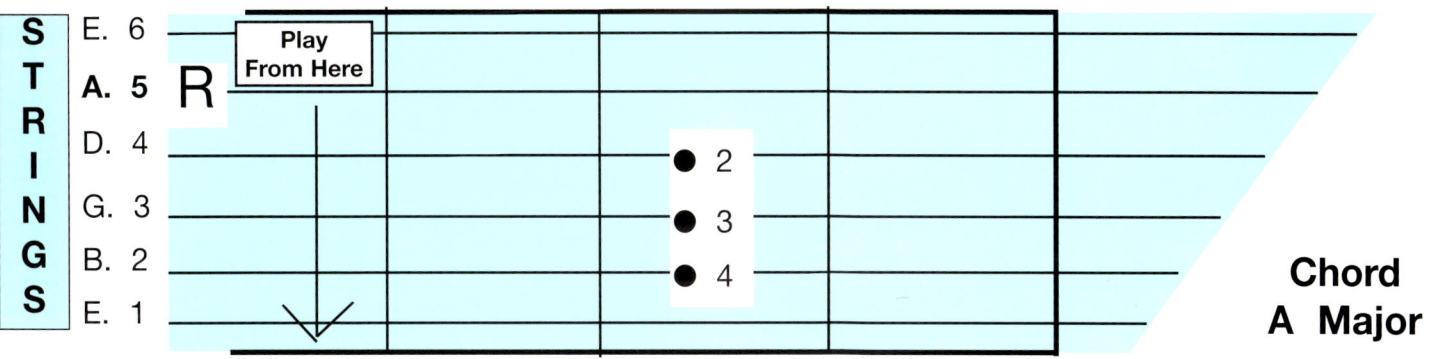

Start playing from the string which contains the **R** and continue to the bottom string as in the D Major chord here.

The string with the **R** is called the **ROOT NOTE** of the chord it will be the same note (D) as the chord (D) you are playing and will vary from chord to chord. (Important) You cannot hit the strings above the **R** while playing a Chord.

See example here for the **A Major Chord** playing from the **A String**

IMPORTANT

If you write and do most activities with your right hand, then you will play the guitar using right chord positions as above and on the following right hand page columns only.

9

Chords For LEFT HANDED Players Only

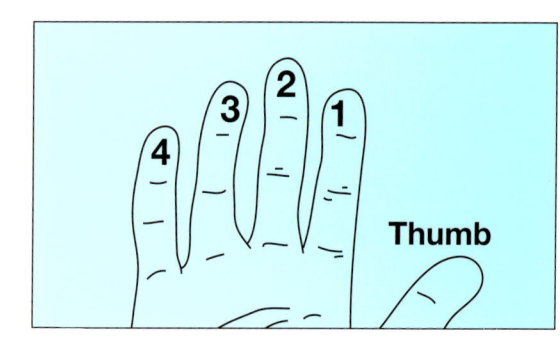

STRINGS: E A D G B E

R (1st Fret, 2nd Fret)
- 2nd fret, D string: finger 2
- 2nd fret, G string: finger 3
- 2nd fret, B string: finger 4

A Major

Root Note R
- 1st fret, B string: finger 1
- 2nd fret, D string: finger 2
- 2nd fret, G string: finger 3

A Minor

R
- 2nd fret, D string: finger 2
- 2nd fret, B string: finger 3

A 7

Correct Holding Position for **Left Handed** Guitar

10

1
2
3
4
Thumb

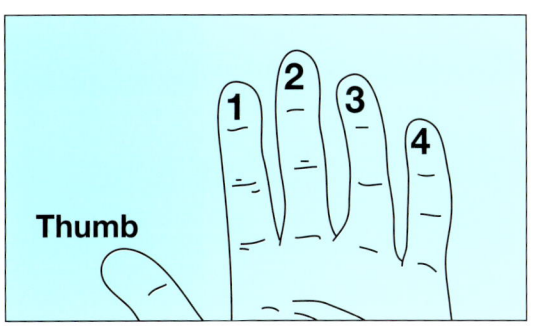

Chords For RIGHT HANDED Players Only

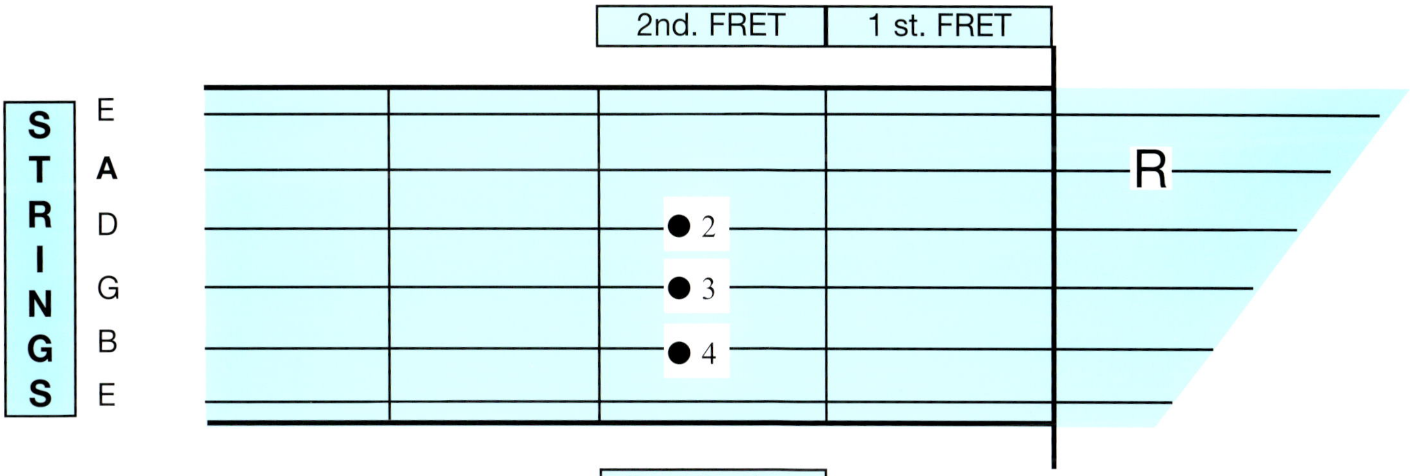

2nd. FRET
1 st. FRET
STRINGS
E
A
D
G
B
E
R
2
3
4

A Major

Root Note
R
2
3
1

A Minor

R
2
3

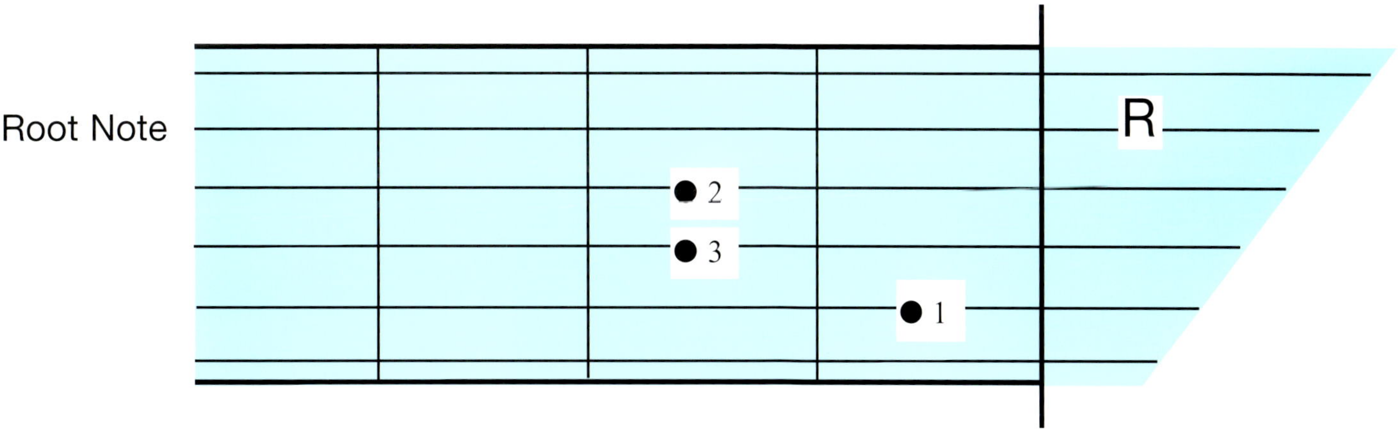

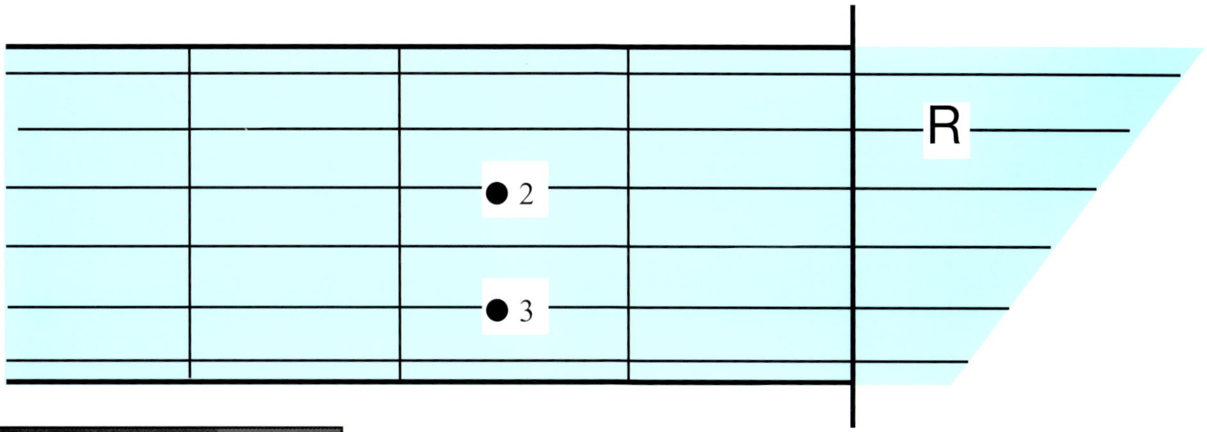

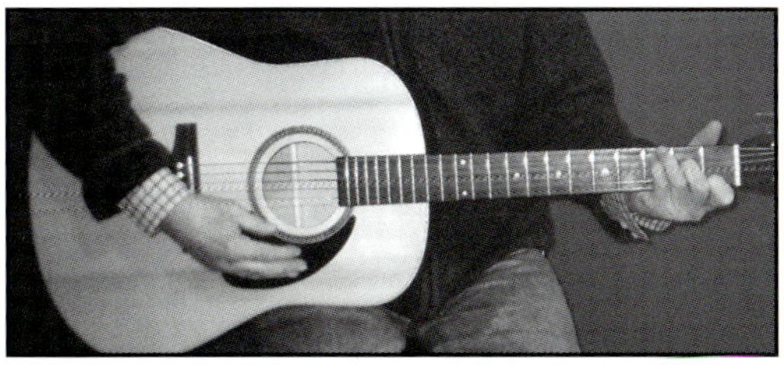

Correct Holding Position for **Right Handed** Guitar

A 7

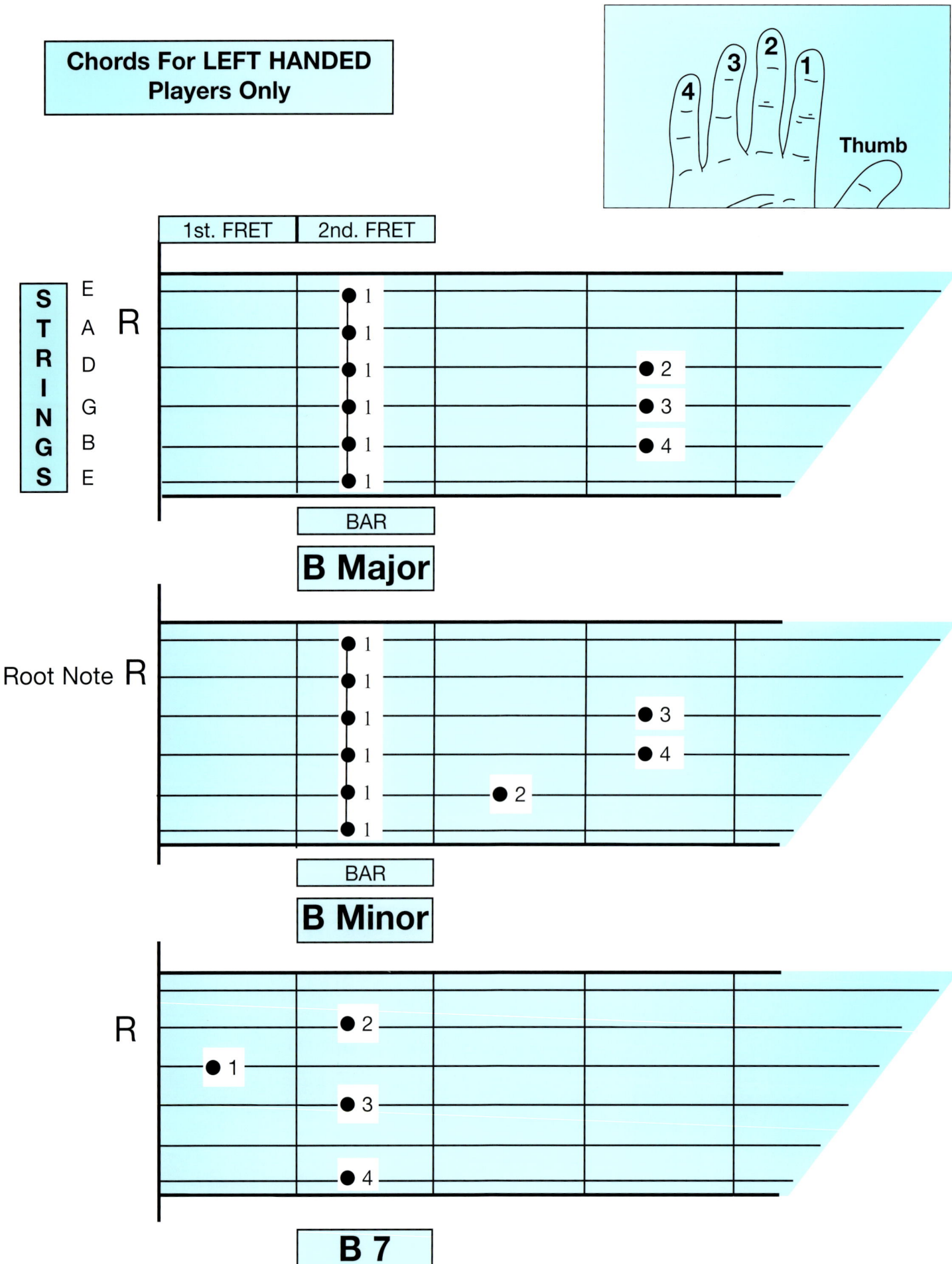

For B Major and B Minor - bar the second fret with your first finger

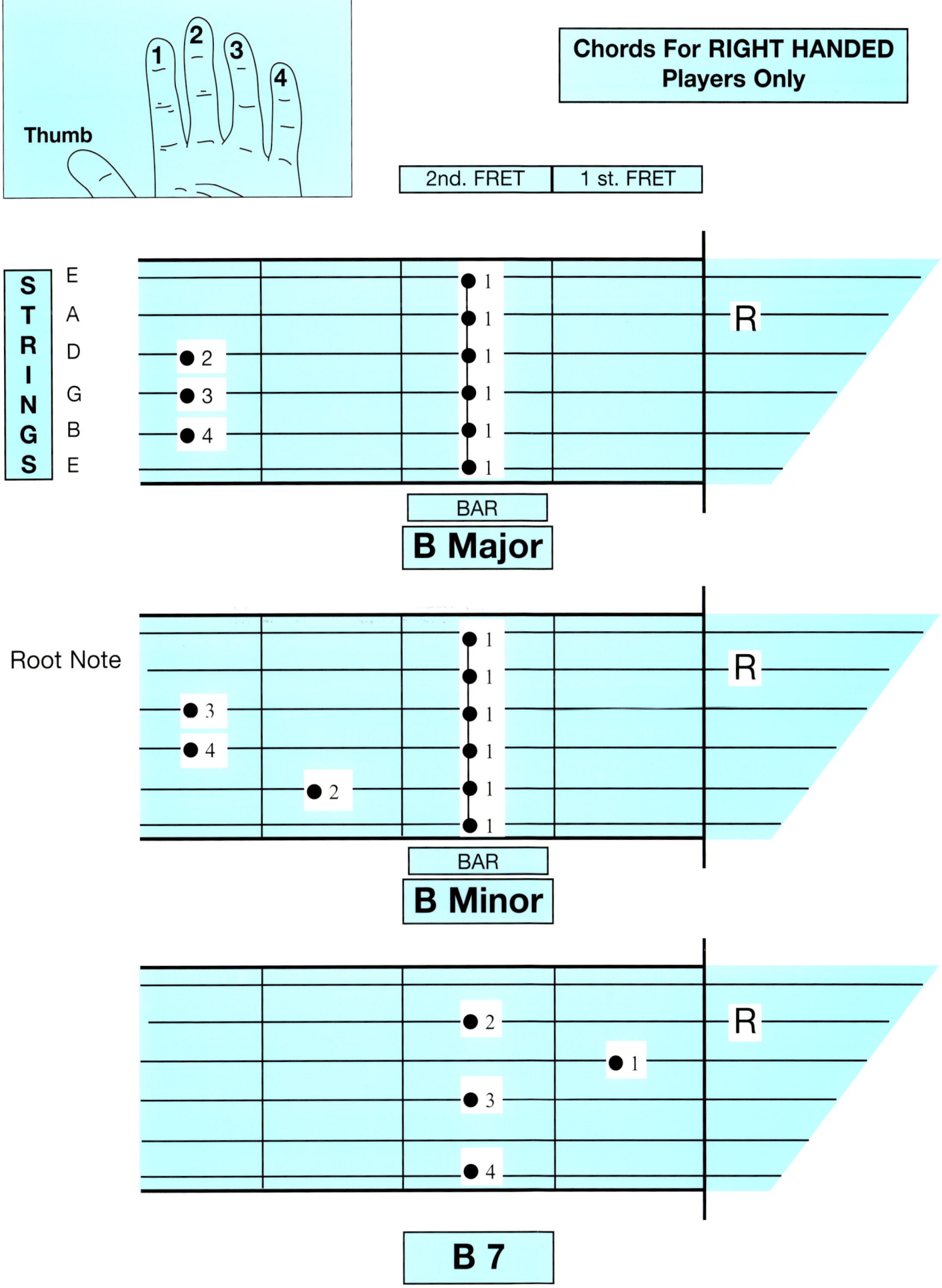

For B Major and B Minor - bar the second fret with your first finger

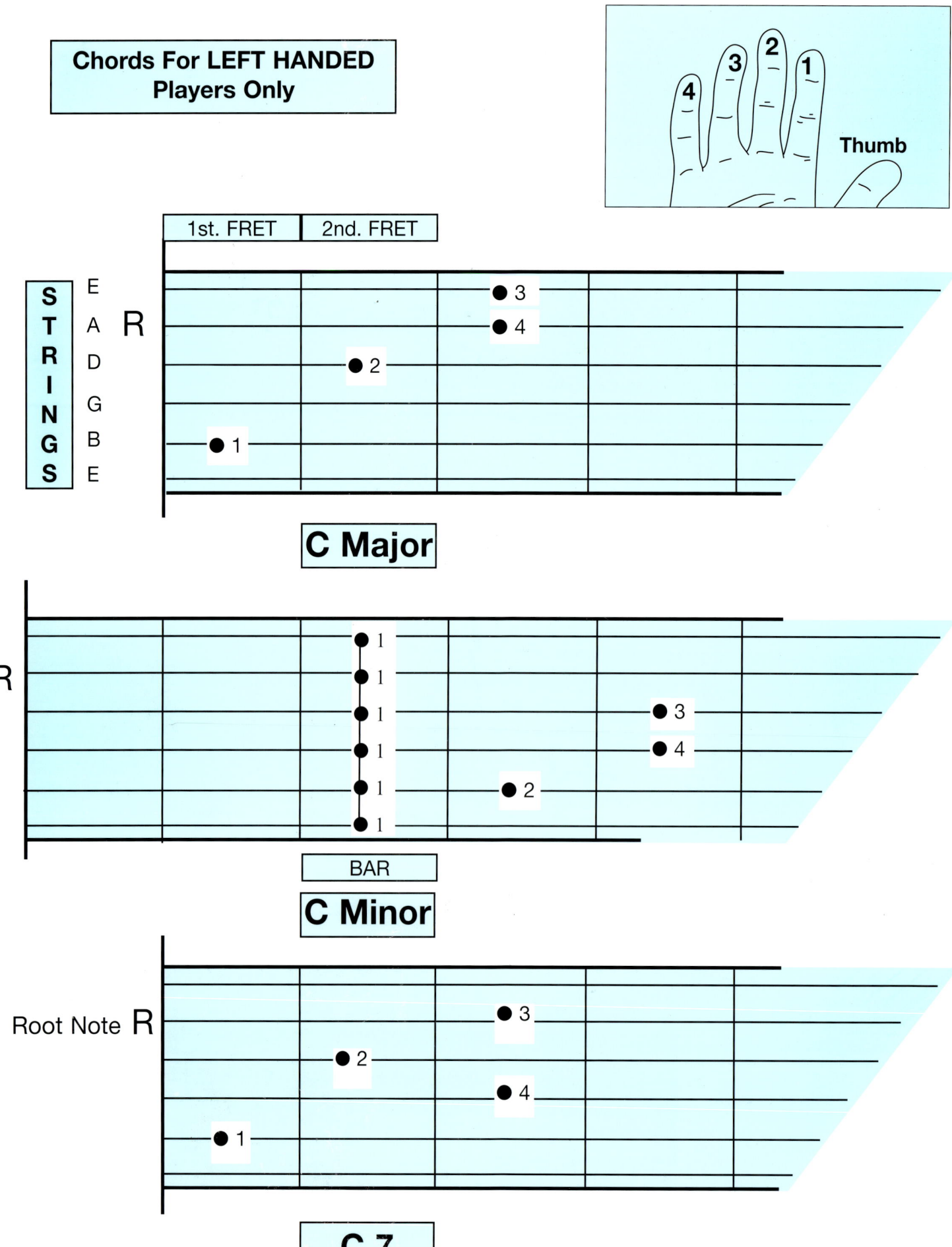

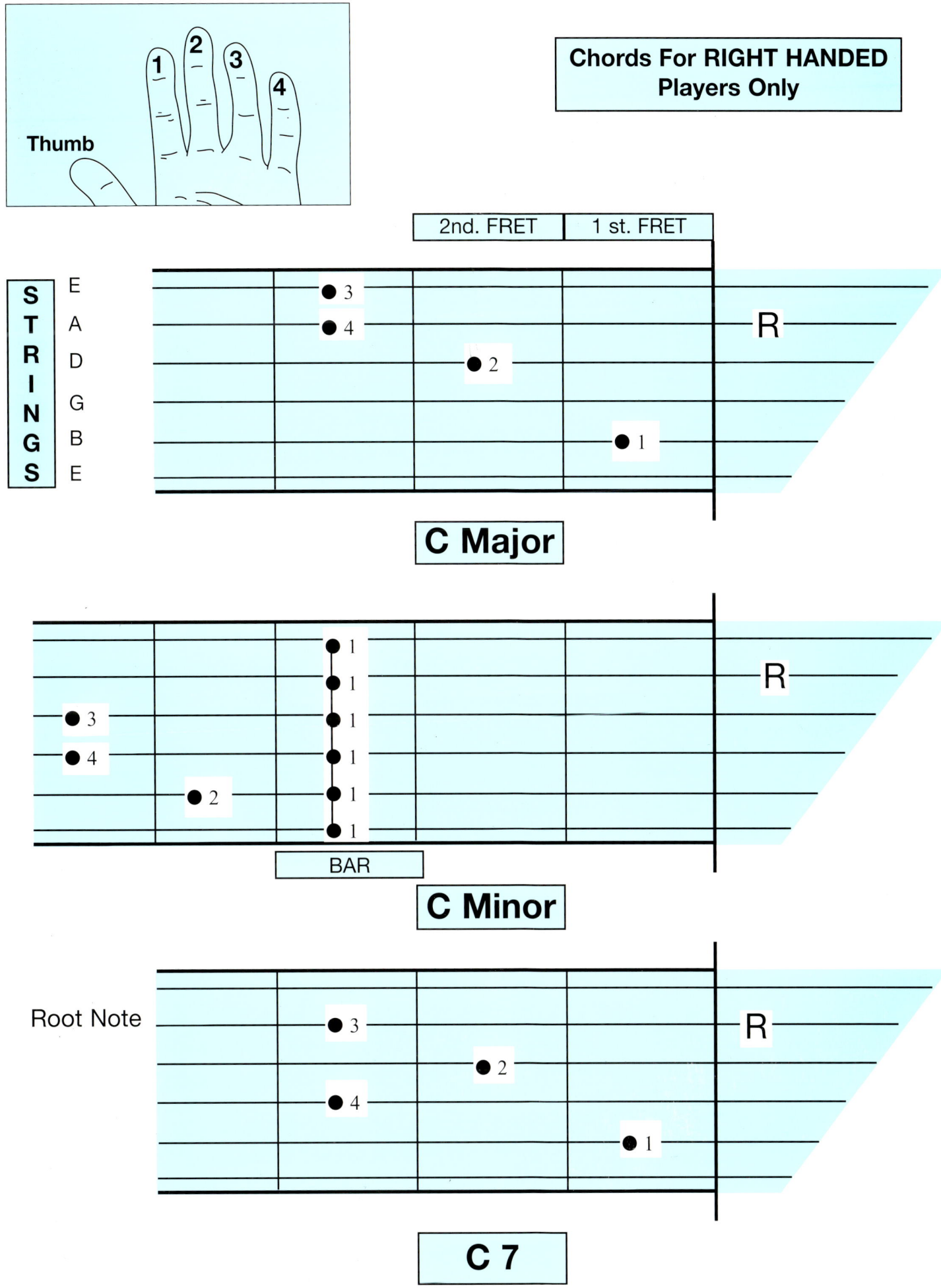

For C Minor - bar the third fret with your first finger

Chords For LEFT HANDED Players Only

4
3
2
1
Thumb

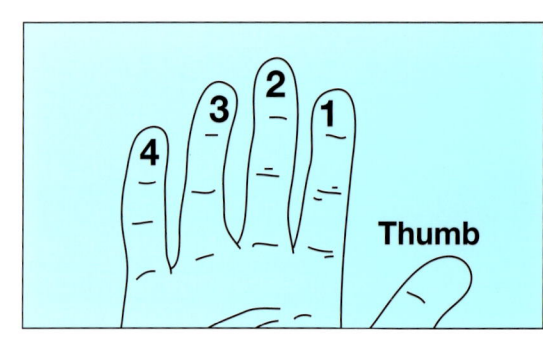

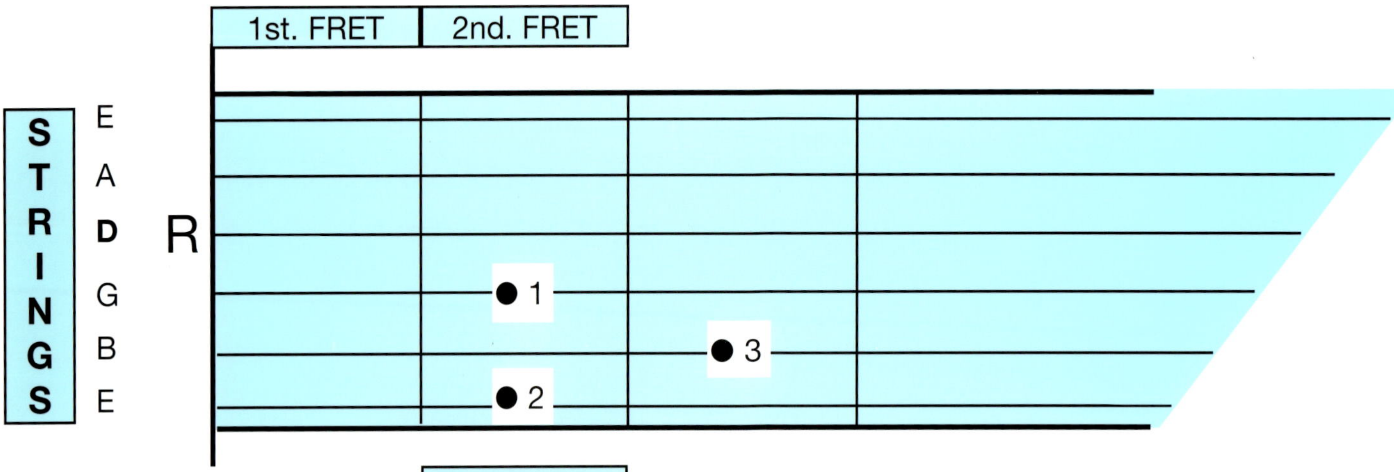

1st. FRET
2nd. FRET
STRINGS
E
A
D
G
B
E
R
1
3
2

D Major

Root Note R
2
3
1

D Minor

R
2
1
3

D 7

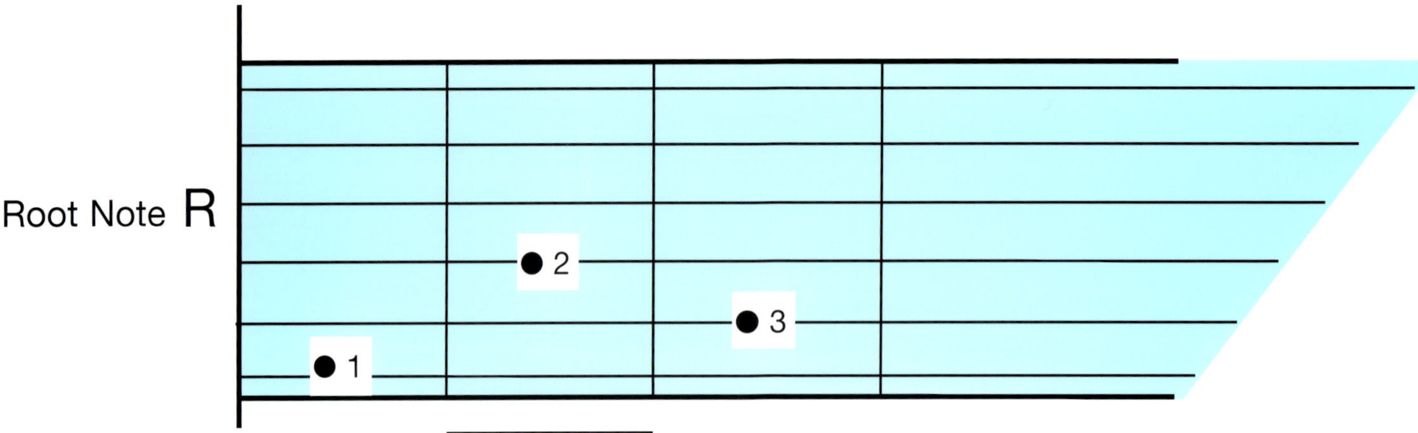

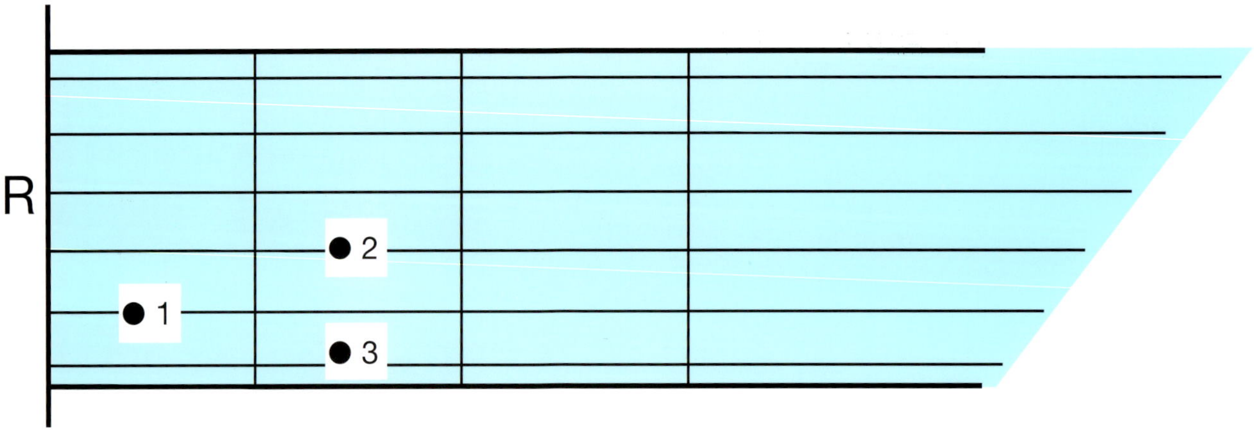

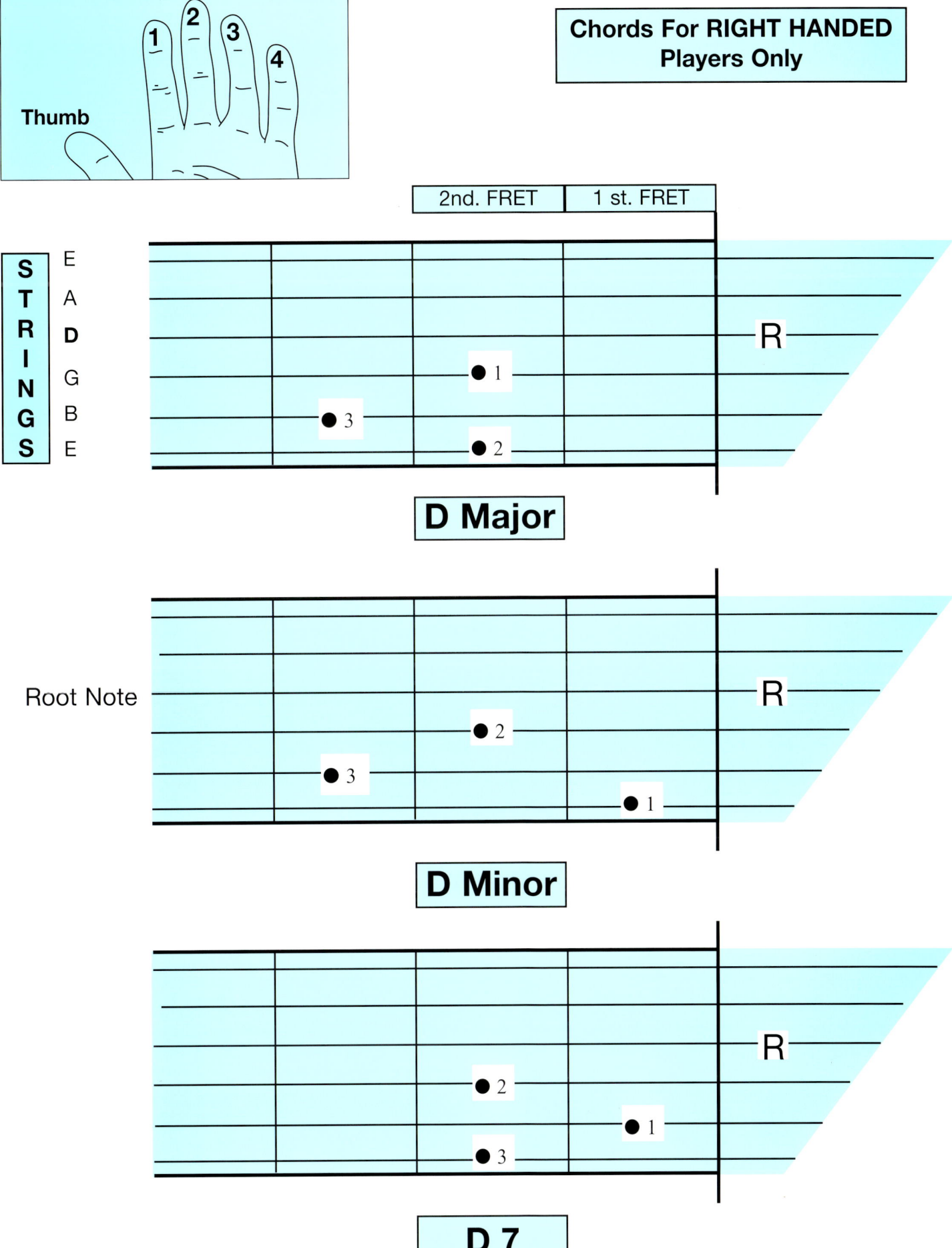

Chords For LEFT HANDED Players Only

4
3
2
1
Thumb

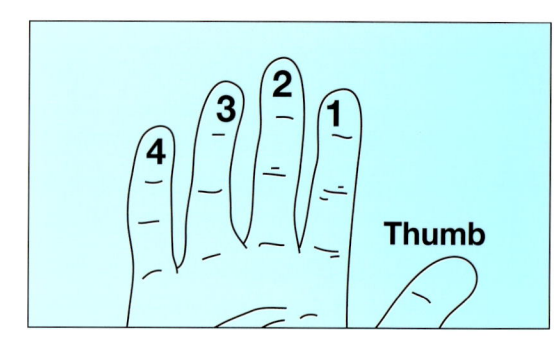

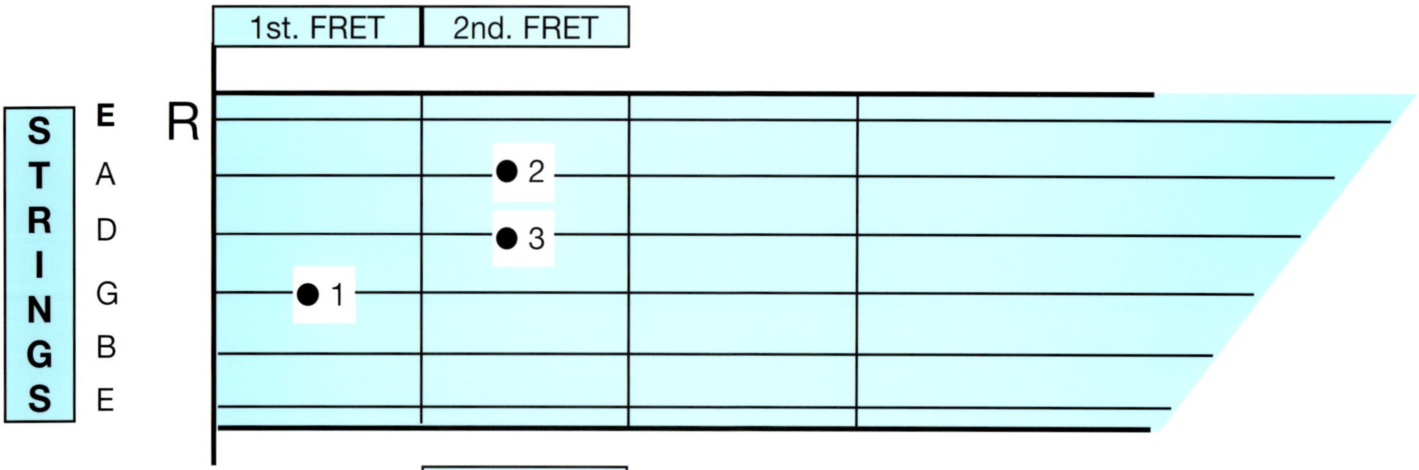

1st. FRET
2nd. FRET
STRINGS
E
A
D
G
B
E
R
2
3
1

E Major

Root Note R
2
3

E Minor

R
2
3
1
4

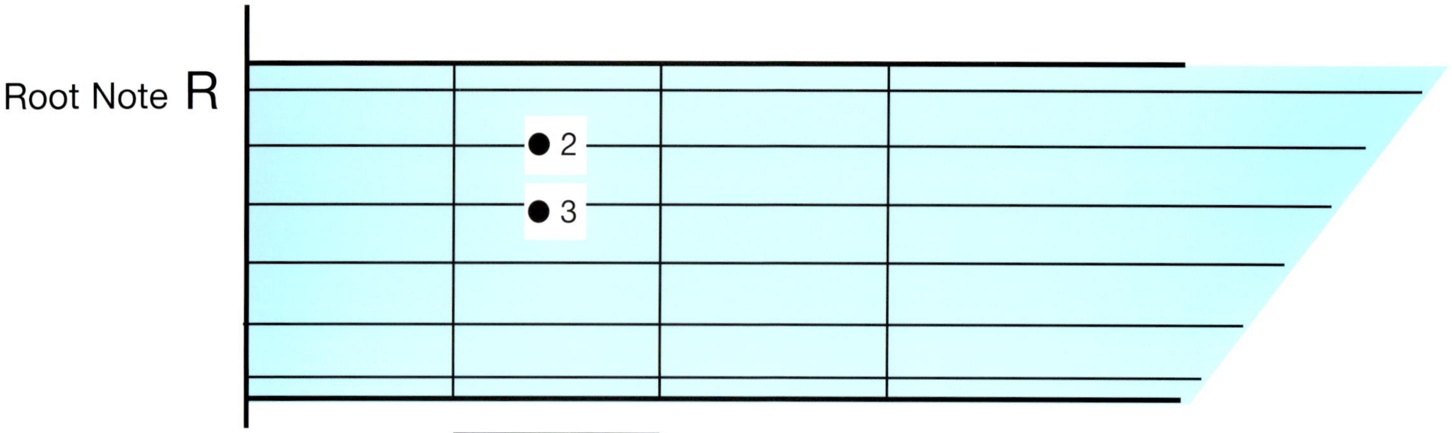

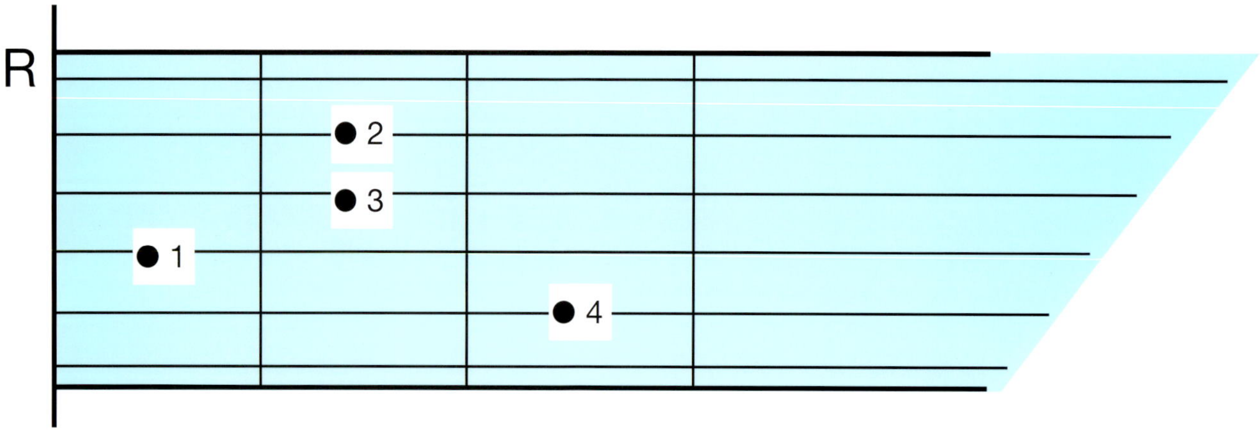

E 7

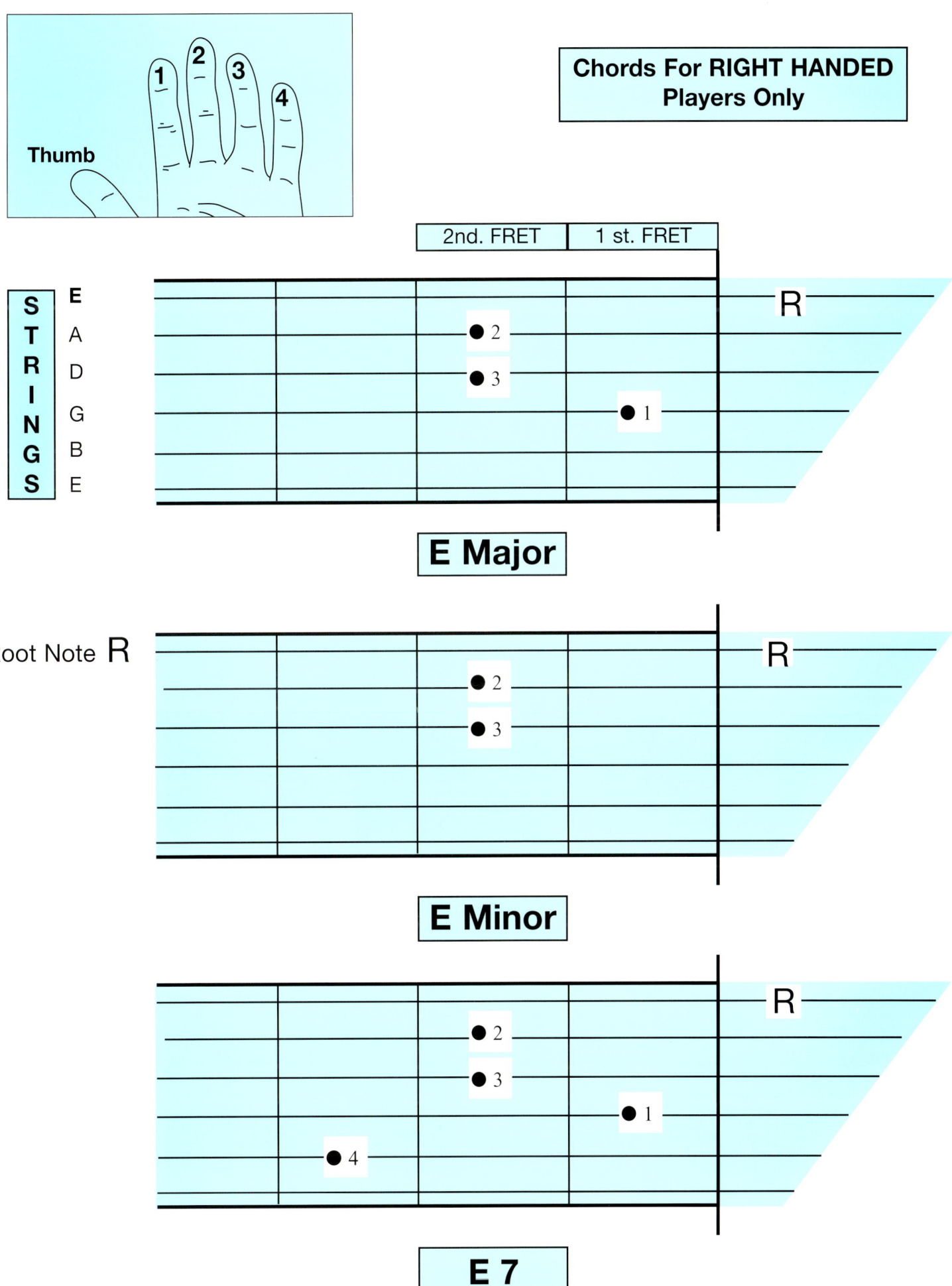

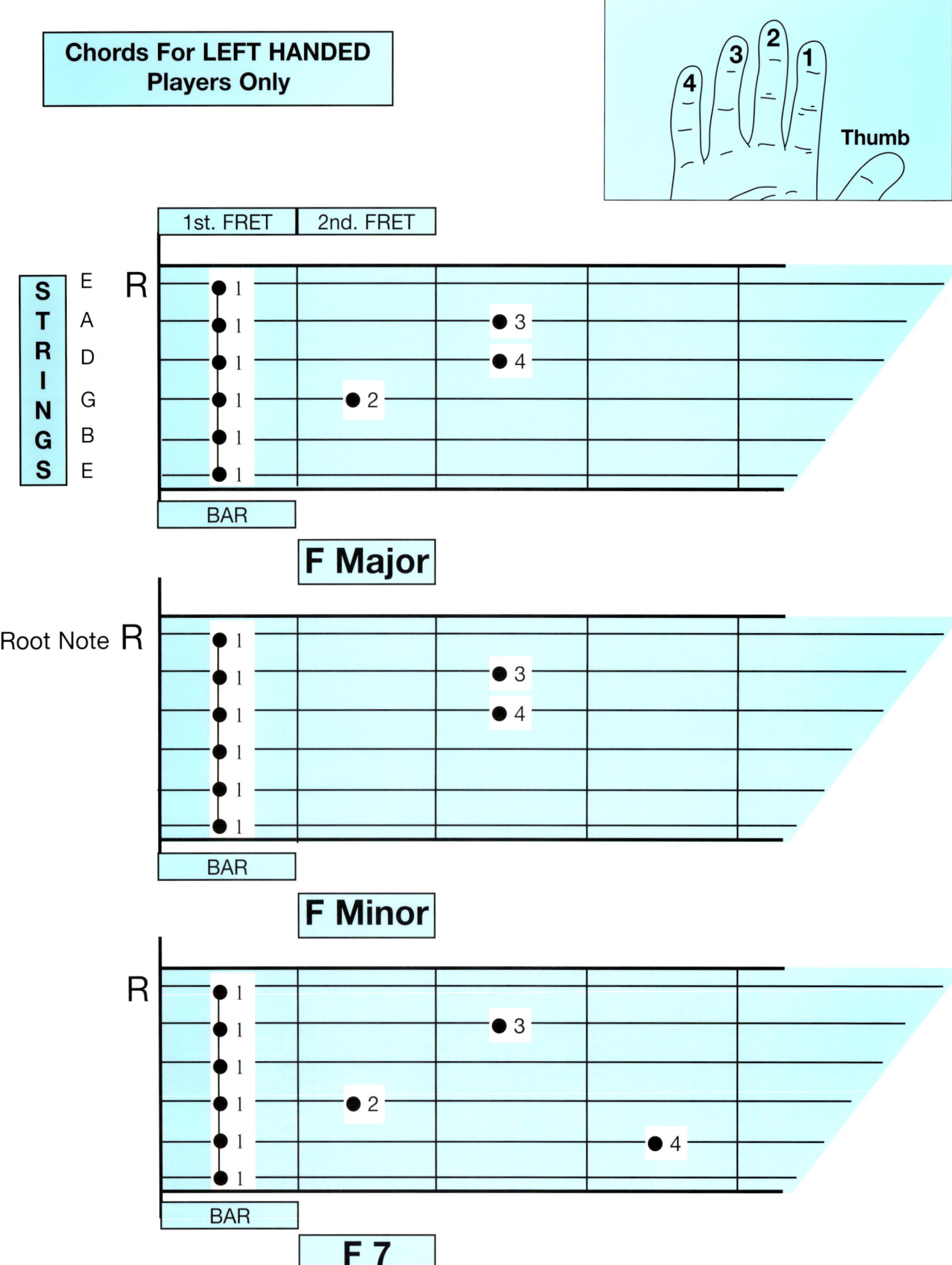

For F Major, F Minor, and F 7 - bar the first fret with your first finger

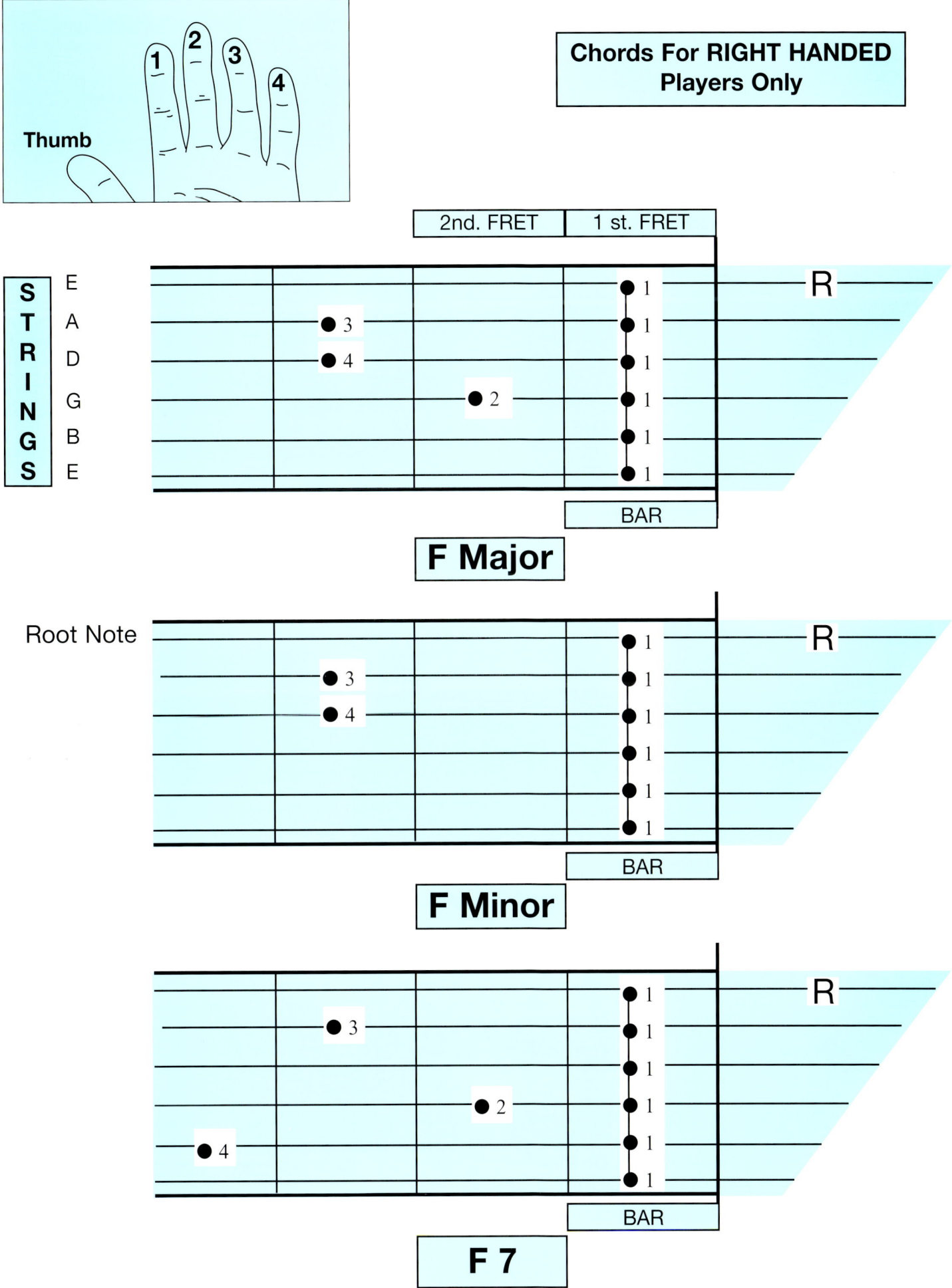

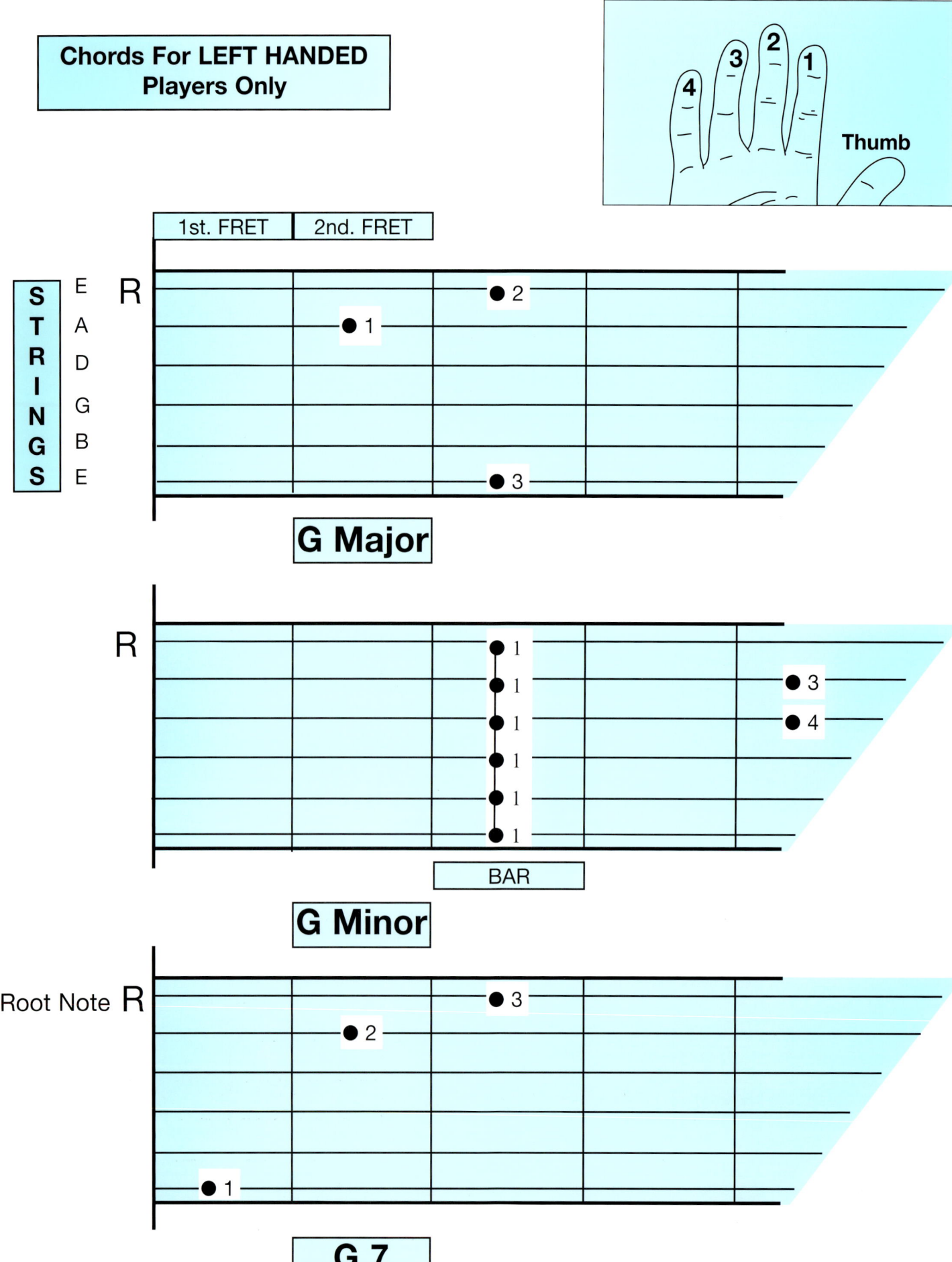

For G Minor - bar the third fret with your first finger

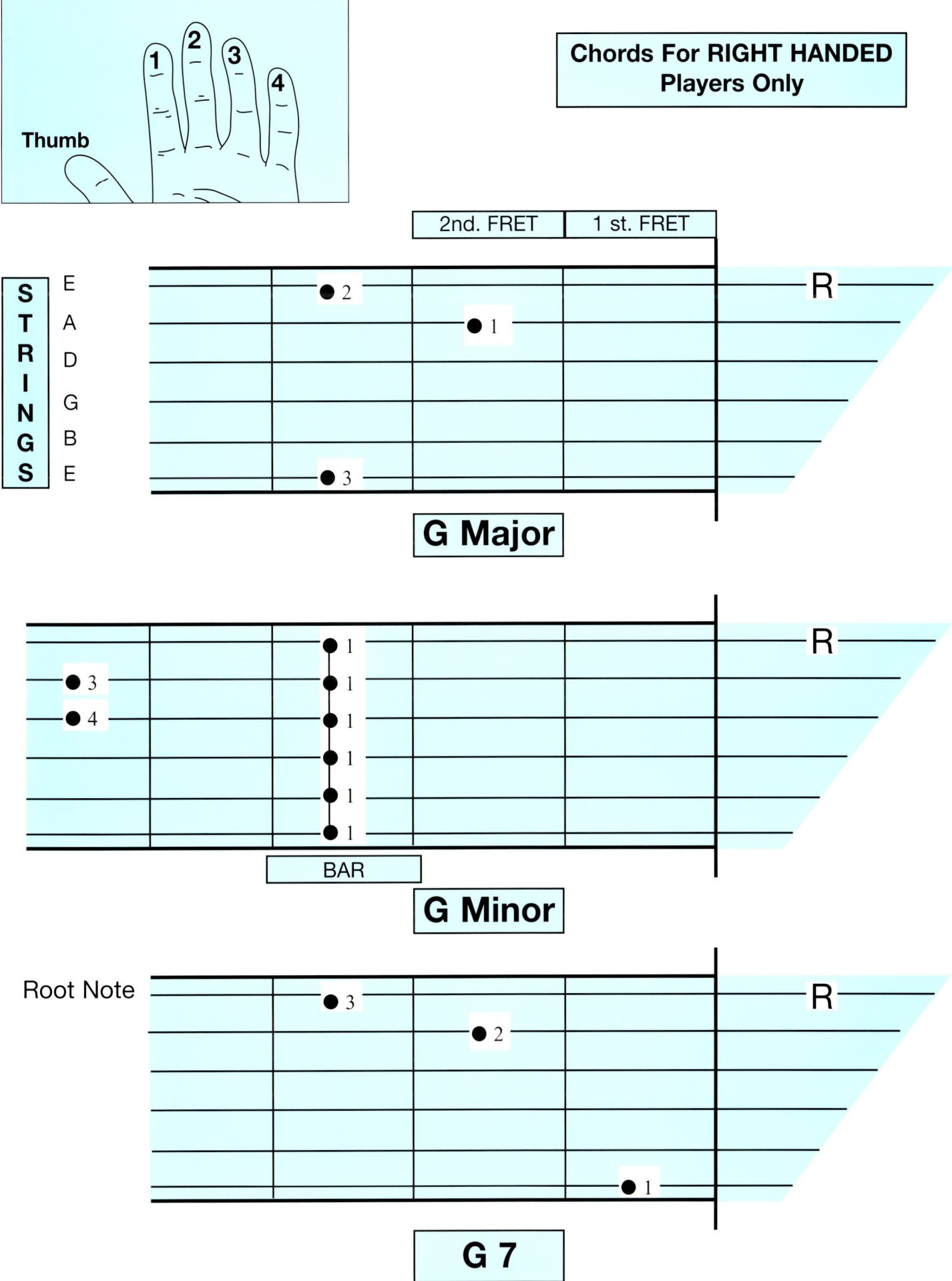

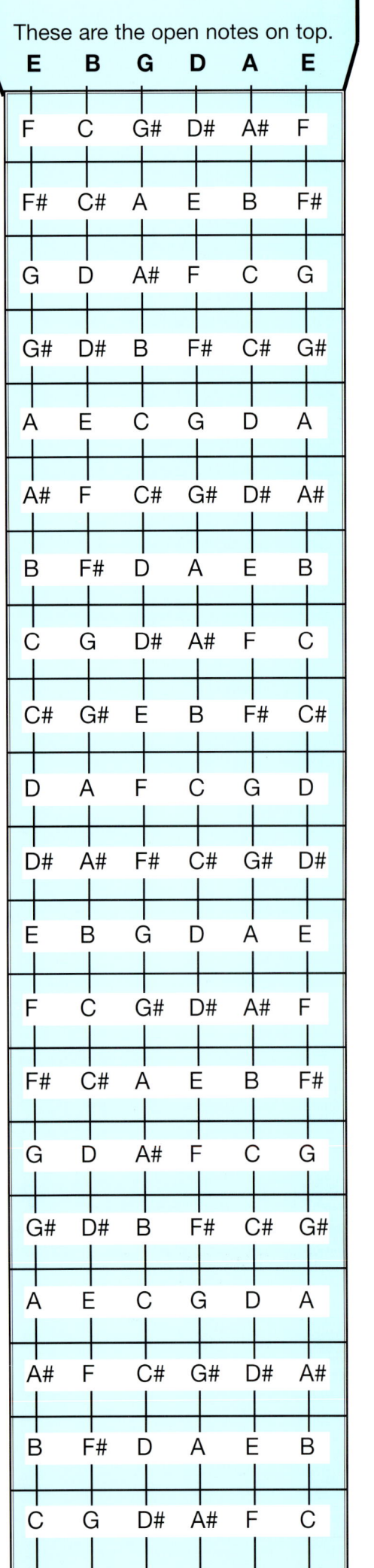

Fret Board

These are the open notes on top.

E	B	G	D	A	E	Fret
F	C	G#	D#	A#	F	1st. Fret.
F#	C#	A	E	B	F#	2nd.
G	D	A#	F	C	G	3rd.
G#	D#	B	F#	C#	G#	4th.
A	E	C	G	D	A	5
A#	F	C#	G#	D#	A#	6
B	F#	D	A	E	B	7
C	G	D#	A#	F	C	8
C#	G#	E	B	F#	C#	9
D	A	F	C	G	D	10
D#	A#	F#	C#	G#	D#	11
E	B	G	D	A	E	12
F	C	G#	D#	A#	F	13
F#	C#	A	E	B	F#	14
G	D	A#	F	C	G	15
G#	D#	B	F#	C#	G#	16
A	E	C	G	D	A	17
A#	F	C#	G#	D#	A#	18
B	F#	D	A	E	B	19
C	G	D#	A#	F	C	20

These are the notes that you get when you place a finger in any position on the Fret board and play as a single note all the way up to the 20th. Fret ↓

Left Handed Guitar

This Chart shows all the individual notes from the open strings right up to the 20th fret.

You can see that there is a structure to the continuation of the notes from A to G# sharp.

On there own when played or plucked, the sound will give a single note sound.

The open notes at the top are the notes you get when plucked without putting any finger on the fret board, and when tuned properly will give the sounds from the thickest string to the narrowest

E. B. G. D. A. E.

The notes will follow up the fret board as.

A
A# (Sharp)
B (No Sharp)
C
C# (Sharp)
D
D# (Sharp)
E (No Sharp)
F
F# (Sharp)
G
G# (Sharp)

A Sharp note is a half note that follows the full note for example A is followed by A# (sharp) which is a sound half way between the notes A and B. C and D and so on.

You will notice that some of these notes do not have a sharp note following them, this is because B & E notes do not have a sharp note or (half Note) following them, they go directly to the next full note.

Its the same with the chords, B & E chords do not have sharp chords, all the rest do.
(Covered in Book 2.)

Right Handed Guitar

These are the open notes on top.

E	A	D	G	B	E	Fret
F	A#	D#	G#	C	F	1st. Fret.
F#	B	E	A	C#	F#	2nd.
G	C	F	A#	D	G	3rd.
G#	C#	F#	B	D#	G#	4th.
A	D	G	C	E	A	5
A#	D#	G#	C#	F	A#	6
B	E	A	D	F#	B	7
C	F	A#	D#	G	C	8
C#	F#	B	E	G#	C#	9
D	G	C	F	A	D	10
D#	G#	C#	F#	A#	D#	11
E	A	D	G	B	E	12
F	A#	D#	G#	C	F	13
F#	B	E	A	C#	F#	14
G	C	F	A#	D	G	15
G#	C#	F#	B	D#	G#	16
A	D	G	C	E	A	17
A#	D#	G#	C#	F	A#	18
B	E	A	D	F#	B	19
C	F	A#	D#	G	C	20

These are the notes that you get when you place a finger in any position on the Fret board and play as a single note all the way up to the 20th. Fret ↓

This Chart shows all the individual notes from the open strings right up to the 20th fret.
You can see that there is a structure to the continuation of the notes from A to G# sharp.
On there own when played or plucked, the sound will give a single note sound.
The open notes at the top are the notes you get when plucked without putting any finger on the fret board, and when tuned properly will give the sounds from the thickest string to the narrowest

E. A. D. G. B. E.

The notes will follow up the fret board as.
A
A# (Sharp)
B (No Sharp)
C
C# (Sharp)
D
D# (Sharp)
E (No Sharp)
F
F# (Sharp)
G
G# (Sharp)

A Sharp note is a half note that follows the full note for example A is followed by A# (sharp) which is a sound half way between the notes A and B. C and D and so on.
You will notice that some of these notes do not have a sharp note following them, this is because B & E notes do not have a sharp note or (half Note) following them, they go directly to the next full note.

Its the same with the chords,
B & E chords do not have sharp chords, all the rest do.
(Covered in Book 2.)

25

Strumming

Strumming is when you strike with your thumb or plec over the strings from the root note to the bottom string and sometimes back to the root note depending on the song and strumming pattern that you are playing. We strum by either using our thumb or a plectrum (plec) from the Greek word *Plektron* meaning to hit or to strike. We strum to songs using strum patterns, depending on the type of song we are playing.

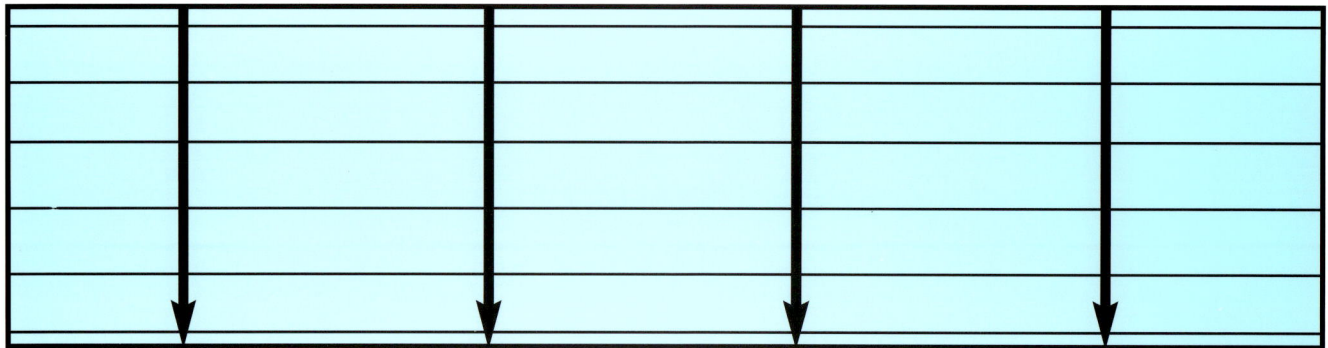

The above strumming pattern consists of four down strikes with equal time space between each down strum. This particular pattern is used mainly for slower songs.

Below the strumming pattern consists of one full down strike, one full up, one full down, one full up and finish with one full down, equal time space between each strum. (*Remember you must not hit the strings above the* **(R) ROOT NOTE** *of the chord you are playing.*)

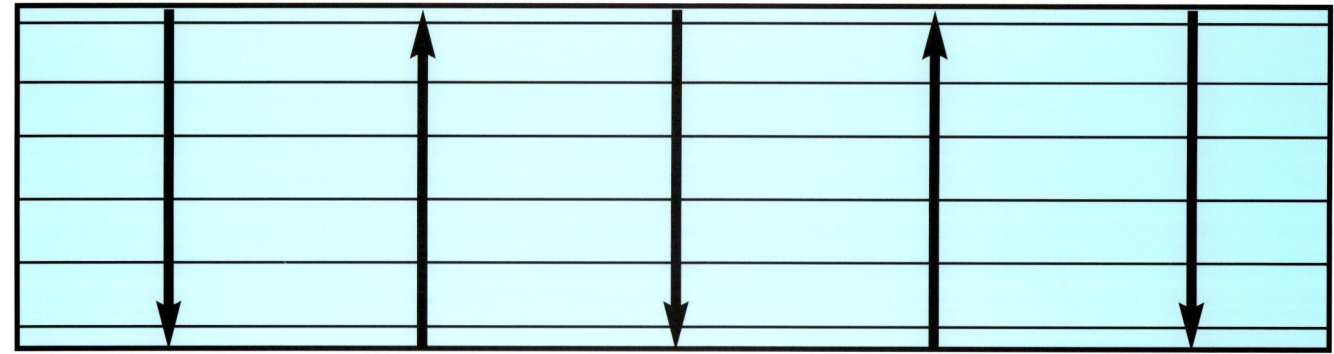

As you can see below, the strumming pattern is different again. Example: If you are playing an A Chord, tip the A String followed by two full down strikes. Tip the A String again followed by two more full down strikes. When you are finished, the whole cycle starts all over again, so you get a continuous sound. If you are playing a D Chord, tip the D String followed by two full down strikes etc.

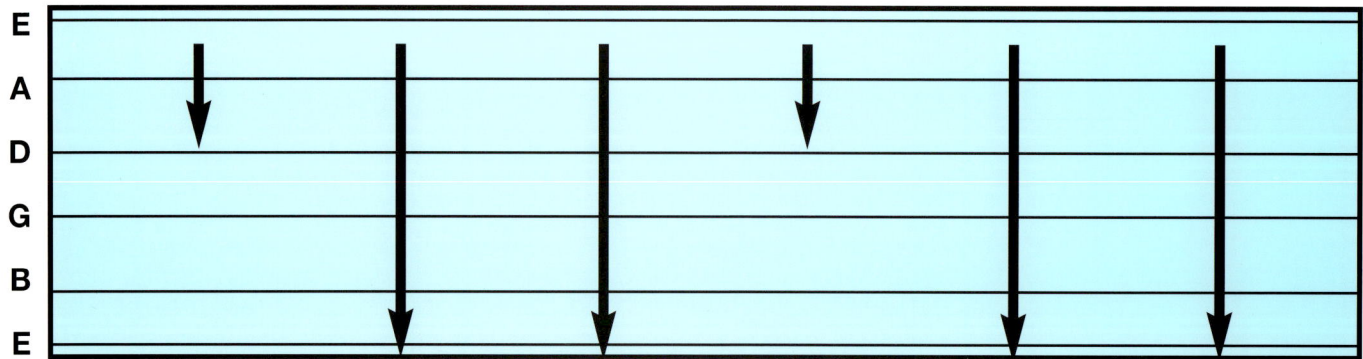

Be consistent in your strumming cycle, avoid leaving a pause unless there is a larger gap between the arrows.

Correct Holding Position for **Left Handed** Guitar

Correct Holding Position for **Right Handed** Guitar

Now that you have an understanding of how the Guitar works and a knowledge of basic chords, its time to purchase from your music shop a good **chord song book** of popular songs. You will not know every single chord of every song but you will have covered most of them. Try putting what you have learned so far into practice.

Relax with your Guitar and enjoy it.
See You In Book 2

A Special thanks to Caroline & Joe at Martello Press
and to Joan & Brendan Gogan (Slane) for all your help & support.

NOTES